PENPALS *for* Handwriting

Year 3 Practice Book (7–8 years)

By **Gill Budgell & Kate Ruttle**

Supported by the
National Handwriting Association
Promoting good practice

Contents

CAMBRIDGE UNIVERSITY PRESS

Practise the joins.

 mus ic ian sev en

Write the words.

 musician seven crane

Write the sentence.

 We can see seven musicians
in a row on a crane.

Practise the pattern.

c ov er

cover

mem or ise

memorise

s ci ence

science

2

Practise the joins.

ll   ll   ll   tt   tt   tt

Write the words.

Hello little balloon

Write the joke.

*What did the little balloon
say to the pin?*

"Hello Buster!"

Practise the pattern.

**Read and write
the words.**

c all ed

called

p add led

paddled

ti ck led

tickled

3

Practise the joins.

 sh　　　sl　　　st　　　sk

Write the words.

 ship　　　slip　　　sting　　　skin

Make compound words by joining words from each box.

ship	chop
paint	skate
milk	star

brush	fish
wreck	shake
stick	board

Practise the pattern.

should

star

finish

skeleton

friendship

Practise the joins.

 _sw si se sm sn sp su_

Write the words.

 submarine   secret   submit

Write the report.

> Sensational news story
> Yesterday, a secret supersonic
> submarine submerged in the
> Irish Sea. Is it on a spying
> mission?

Read and write the words.

surprise

smiles

snorkel

sister

university

Practise the pattern.

∫ ∫ ∫ ∫ ∫ ∫ ∫ ∫

Practise the joins.

sa   sc   sd   sg   so   sq

Write the words.

sensational   disguises   squash

Write the poster.

Disguises for sale:

scary squirrel
wise scientist
sad stegosaurus
awesome spaceman

Practise the pattern.

Read and write the words.

wisdom

square

biscuit

Wednesday

safari

6

Practise the joins.

rb   rh   rk   rl   rt

Write the words.

sparkling   *whirling*   *flirting*

Write the poem.

Sparkling, the leaves
Whirl and twirl
Curl and swirl
Flirting in the wind

Practise the pattern.

7

Read and write the words.

dart

spark

rhythm

early

harbour

Practise the joins.

ri   ru   rn   rp

Write the words.

surprise   descriptions

Write the poster.

*the rising sun
a burning carpet
a charity run
an April shower*

Describe these pictures for a friend to draw.

Practise the pattern.

8

Read and write the words.

rice

turnip

runner

chorus

purpose

Practise the joins.

 _ra   rd   rg   ro_

Write the words.

 orange   emergency   survival

Write the question.

 In an emergency, would you
make a cardboard raft?

 Oh rats!
I'm drowning!

Practise the pattern.

Read and write the words.

board

round

afraid

circle

argument

Practise the joins.

are　ere　ure　ore　ire

Write the words.

feature　adventures

Write the poster.

Treasure Island
Pirates Galore

Showing here for one week only.

Pre-book directly online
or here at The Spire Theatre.

**Read and write
the words.**

core

measure

parents

increase

remember

Practise the pattern.

eee eee eee

Practise the letters.

 g j y f b p q x z

Write the words.

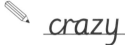 crazy   pen   breaks

Write the rules.

Break letters

We do not join from break letters.
Most break letters end with a
pencil stroke to the left;
x and z never join.

Practise the pattern.

bigger

breakfast

jogger

mystery

injured

Practise the joins.

if   ef   af   of

Write the words.

aircraft   safe   refuel

Write the letter. Put the parts in order.

This afternoon I took the book to the local airfield.

Dear Grandfather

Thank you for the book on aircraft. I'm very grateful for it.

Hopefully, we will see you soon. Lots of love Alfie

Read and write the words.

often

prefer

proof

terrified

spacecraft

Practise the pattern.

ſ ſ ſ ſ ſ ſ ſ ſ

Practise the joins.

 fl fl fl ft ft ft

Write the words.

 flash flood inflatables

Write the sentences.

Terrible flash floods have affected families living here. Elderly people were airlifted from rooftops this afternoon. Others are still afloat on rafts and inflatable dingies.

Practise the pattern.

Read and write the words.

flag

lift

flavour

soften

camouflage

Practise the joins.

 _fe   fi   fu   fr   fy_

Write the words.

 five   funny   friends

Write the sentences. Fill the gaps with your friends' names.

 My friends are wonderful.

_____ _is funny._
_____ _is confident._
_____ _is fearless._
_____ _is friendly._

Practise the pattern.

 Read and write the words.

film

frill

life

satisfy

certificate

Practise the joins.

 fo   fo   fa   fa

Write the words.

 four facts for you to fathom

Write the sentences. Write *fact* **or** *fiction* **after each.**

 The first fossil was found last Friday.
A firefighter wears a uniform.
A fox leaves no footprints

Practise the pattern.

Read and write the words.

forwards

farm

surface

before

information

15

Practise the joins.

 ff   ff   ff   ff

Write the words.

 toffee   waffle   coffee

Write the dialogue.

 "Can I offer you a toffee or a waffle?" Effie asked Asiff. "Both affect me badly and I'd be sniffling and snuffling."

Practise the pattern.

Read and write the words.

offer

afford

traffic

difficult

scaffolding

Practise the joins.

 rr   rr   rr   rr

Write the words.

 hurry   carry   flurry

Write the address.

Harriet Carrington
The Old Barracks
7 Barracuda Parade
Quarry Hill Estate
Torrenton Barretteshire
SM7 8RR

Read and write the words.

burrow

carry

horrible

quarrel

gooseberries

Practise the pattern.

17

Practise the joins.

 ss   ss   ss   ss

Write the words.

 criss-cross   loss   hiss

Write the sentence.

 The harmless snake hissed
breathlessly as it
criss-crossed over
the mossy wilderness.

Practise the pattern.

**Read and write
the words.**

unless

cross

address

princess

impossible

Practise the joins.

 qu   qu   qu   qu

Write the words.

 quiz   question   quick

Write the quiz. Answer the questions.

 1. Must all the faces of a cube be equal-sized squares?

2. Can a square be a quarter of a quadrilateral?

3. Continue this sequence: 3, 6, 9 ...

Practise the pattern.

quack

quite

quiet

liquid

earthquake

Practise the joins.

ly ily ally ly ily ally

Write the words.

merrily   hilly   diagonally

Write the words. Keep your down strokes parallel.

lightly   gloomily   kindly

cheerfully   wonderfully   funnily

Write each in a sentence.

Practise the pattern.

Write the rhyme.

Patiently, the fisherman waits.
Will he catch...
A mattress spring or welly boot?
A croquet mallet, a wooden flute?
A pirate's earring, a buffalo's fleece?
Or just a moment
for quiet and peace?

Read and write
the words.

asked

demanded

requested

wished

commanded

Practise the pattern.

Write the heading.

Dialogue jokes

Write the joke. Check your letters are evenly spaced.
Check your apostrophe has a letter space.

"Doctor, doctor, I think I'm a dog!" cried the patient.

"Sit on the couch and we'll talk about it," soothed the doctor.

"But I'm not allowed on the couch!" barked the patient.

they're

we'll

we're

it's

should've

Practise the pattern.

Write the heading.

Where are the Poles?

Write the text. Allow space for one or two letter os between each word.

The North Pole is the point on Earth that is the furthest north. It is found in the middle of the Arctic Ocean. The South Pole is furthest south. It is near the centre of the continent called Antarctica.

Practise the pattern.

Read and write the words.

heading

sub-heading

paragraph

sentence

clause

Write the heading.

Are your LETTERS .... cap height

the same size? .... Lower case x
height letters

Draw the table. Write the words in the table.

Word class	Punctuation mark	Type of sentence

command *adverb*

apostrophe *comma*

noun *adjective*

Practise the pattern.

vowel

consonant

alphabet

letter

twenty-six

24

Write the heading.

 Fire ⋯⋯⋯ Check that your writing
is round and flowing

Write the poem.

 "Fire! Fire!" says Obadiah.
"Where? Where?" says Mrs. Pear.
"Behind the rocks," says Dr. Fox.
"Put it out!" says Mr. Trout.
"I've no bucket,"
says Lord MacTucket.
"Use my shoe,"
says You Know Who.

Practise the pattern.

 ! ! ? ? ! ! ? ? ! !

 **Read and write
the words.**

poem

rhyme

rhythm

verse

title

25

Write the heading.

Keep your downstrokes parallel and the ascenders the same height.

Vocabulary in mathematics

Draw the table. Sort and write the words into two lists.

Words about shapes	Words about numbers

horizontal   circle   estimate
addition   thousand   subtraction
cuboid   vertical

Practise the pattern.

26

Read and write the words.

breathe

address

brilliant

schedule

mathematical

Write the heading.

How many letters?

Keep descenders
the same length.   Keep your downstrokes parallel.

Write the words in order of the number of letters.

beautifully   mystery   knowledge

importantly   although

thoughtful   opposite   impossibility

belief   often   experiment

Practise the pattern.

Read and write
the words.

February

bicycle

eighth

difficulty

camouflaged

Practise the joins.

rs   rs   rs   rs

Write the words.

his   hers   theirs   ours

Write the sentences.

It's hers.

No, it's not yours.

Yes, it's ours.

No, it's theirs.

Read and write the words.

yours

sisters

brothers

theirs

Mrs.

Practise the pattern.

28

Write the heading.

 Break letters.

Write the break letter rules.

 We join to but not from g, j, y, b, p.
We do not join to or from x and z.

Write the text and check your break letters.

 The Wright Brothers
Wilbur and Orville Wright liked
engineering challenges. They owned a
bicycle repair shop. Later, they made a
glider. They put an engine in their glider
and invented the world's first aeroplane.

Practise the pattern.

Read and write the words.

enjoying

brother

above

giggle

alphabet

29

Write the heading.

Fast and fluent

Write the words.

musician   balloon   friendship

stegosaurus   rhythm   adventure

Write the sentence very neatly.

The quick brown fox
jumped over the lazy dog.

Now write the sentence as fast as you can. What happens to your writing when you write very fast?

Review your writing using this checklist.

1. Are there any joins you need to practise?

2. Are your letters the right size (capitals too)?

3. Is the spacing between letters and words good?

4. Are your ascenders and descenders parallel?

5. Did your hand move smoothly over the page as you wrote?

Write the alphabet in capital letters.

A B C D E F G H I J K L M N
O P Q R S T U V W X Y Z

Write the book titles.

'My Criminal Life'
by Robin Banks

'The Ghost Hunters'
by Terry Fied

'Falling Trees'
by Tim Burr

Practise the pattern.

Read and write
the words.

book

title

author

page

chapter

32